HOW TO SURVIVE A TSUNAMI

BY MARNE VENTURA

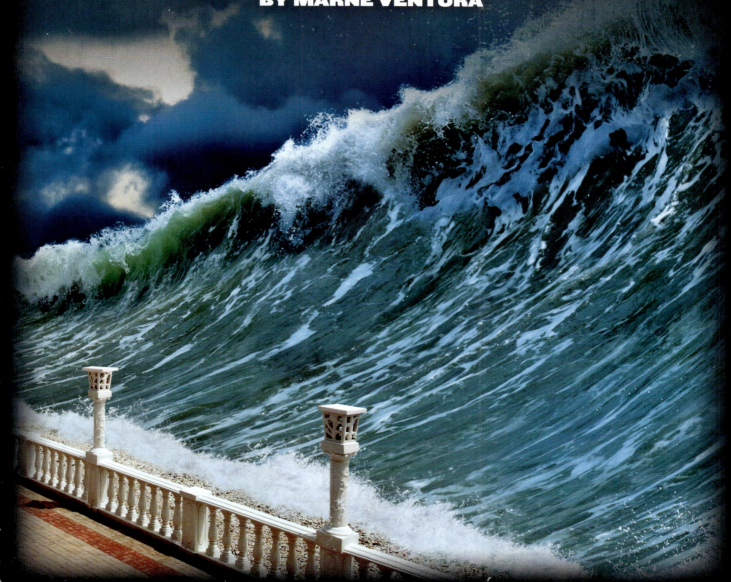

The Child's World®

Published by The Child's World®
1980 Lookout Drive • Mankato, MN 56003-1705
800-599-READ • www.childsworld.com

Acknowledgments
The Child's World®: Mary Berendes, Publishing Director
Red Line Editorial: Editorial direction and production
The Design Lab: Design
Photographs ©: Shutterstock Images, cover, 1, 10, 13, 21;
Steve Photography/Shutterstock Images, 5; Chaiwat
Subprasom/Reuters/Corbis, 6; Koichiri Tezuka-Mainichi
Shimbun/ZumaPress/Newscom, 9; iStockphoto, 15;
A.S. Zain/Shutterstock Images, 17; Stocktrek Images/
Thinkstock, 19

ISBN 9781609731649
LCCN 2014959810

Printed in the United States of America
Mankato, MN
July, 2015
PA02260

ABOUT THE AUTHOR

Marne Ventura is the author of more than 20 books for kids. She loves writing about science, technology, health, and crafts. She also writes stories for children's magazines. Marne and her husband watch for tsunamis on the central coast of California.

TABLE OF CONTENTS

CHAPTER ONE

TSUNAMI!

Tilly Smith walked down the beach with her family. The ten-year-old was on winter break from her school in England. Her family was spending the holiday in Thailand.

Suddenly, Tilly noticed something strange about the ocean. There was a lot of foam on the surface. It looked like the water was bubbling. Tilly had learned about tsunamis at school just two weeks earlier. Her teacher had shown a video about a tsunami in Hawaii. Tilly had learned the warning signs. One was receding water. Another was bubbling and foamy water. She knew everyone on the beach was in danger.

Tilly told her parents a big wave was coming. They did not take her seriously. She became upset. She

When water recedes quickly, it may leave behind lots of foam.

Tilly and her parents speak in Thailand about the dangers of tsunamis.

screamed for everyone to get off the beach. This scared Tilly's younger sister. She went with her father back to the hotel. But Tilly's mother wanted to stay on the beach. Tilly did not want to leave her mother. She knew they needed to get away from the water. Finally, she convinced her mother to leave the beach.

Tilly's father warned the hotel security guards. They got everyone off the beach and into the hotel. People watched from above as a huge wall of water rushed over the beach. It slammed against the building. Tilly helped save more than 100 people because she knew the warning signs of a tsunami.

A 9.0 **magnitude** earthquake in the ocean caused the tsunami in Thailand. Huge walls of water rose up from the **epicenter.** They rolled over the coasts of 11 countries along the Indian Ocean. There was no warning system in place. Most people were surprised by the disaster. Almost 230,000 people died.

The 2004 Indian Ocean tsunami was a rare disaster. Most tsunamis are not so destructive. But they can occur in any ocean. They happen quickly. It makes sense to learn about the dangers tsunamis cause. Disaster might never strike. But having a survival plan could be a lifesaver.

PLATE TECTONICS

The earth's surface is made up of huge pieces called tectonic plates. The plates float on hot rock called the mantle. Heat energy from the mantle makes the plates move. Sometimes two plates bump into each other and stick. As they push harder, energy builds. The edges of the plates finally slip apart. This sends **seismic** waves to the earth's surface that shake the ground. Earthquakes happen near the **faults** between tectonic plates.

CHAPTER TWO

LEARNING THE RISKS

A big tsunami hit Japan's coast in March 2011. It killed more than 18,000 people. The tallest wave was as high as a 12-story building. The water moved toward shore at almost 500 miles per hour (805 km/h). The tsunami destroyed the homes of 452,000 people. It caused a **nuclear** power plant to leak harmful steam. The cost of the damage was $235 billion.

Drowning is the most serious risk in tsunamis. But objects in the moving water can also be dangerous. When a wall of water moves as fast as a jet plane, it can knock over buildings and carry them away. A big tsunami struck Chile in 1960. One survivor remembers seeing houses float away with stoves inside still smoking. This made them look like ships on the water. Big waves

Tsunami waves crash over a neighborhood in Japan on March 11, 2011.

A train in Thailand comes off the tracks following a tsunami in 2004.

can also uproot trees. **Debris** can hit people who are not able to get to high ground.

Tsunami waves can wash away or weaken concrete **foundations**. This can make houses fall down. Standing water can ruin buildings left upright. The moisture can rot wood. Gas and electrical appliances may no longer work. Pipes and sewage systems might break and leak.

Erosion becomes a problem after houses, trees, and roads are carried away. These things help hold the ground in place. Mud and landslides may occur without them. Bridges and highways can break or fall down if the ground under them erodes.

Big waves may disable services and utilities that people count on. There may be no clean water for drinking, cooking, or washing if water pipes break. Broken gas and electric lines mean no power for lights, heat, and appliances. Police stations, fire stations, and hospitals can be damaged. This makes it hard for people to get the help they need.

WHAT HAPPENS DURING A TSUNAMI?

Earthquakes on the ocean floor **displace** the water above. This causes waves to rush away from the quake with tremendous power. The waves slow down and get taller as they get closer to shore. The top of the wave is called the crest. The bottom of the wave is called the trough. The trough acts like a vacuum. It sucks water into the wave, making it bigger. One sign a big wave is coming is when the water by shore gets sucked out.

CHAPTER THREE

SURVIVING THE WAVES

People living on land may not feel a quake many miles away on the ocean floor. So it is important to always be ready. You may have less than two minutes to act by the time you see the first wave. The first rule of tsunami survival is to know if you live in a high-risk area. Big waves smash into coasts. The waves can travel up to a mile (1.6 km) inland. Also, the risk is higher in areas that have had tsunamis in the past.

People in a high-risk area need to know a tsunami's warning signs. This allows them to act quickly. A tsunami may occur if an earthquake near the coast lasts 20 seconds or longer. The water in the sea will go far out. You may even hear a loud noise coming from the ocean. Do not wait to act if you suspect a big wave is

Tsunamis are sometimes called tidal waves. But tsunamis are not related to ocean tides.

WARNING SYSTEMS

Scientists have created ways to warn people before big waves hit. They put sensors on the ocean floor. When a sensor picks up a big wave, it sends a message to a nearby buoy. The buoy sends the message to a satellite. The satellite sends a warning to scientists on land. The scientists then tell officials, who can warn people near the coast. This gives people more time to move to safety.

coming. Do not take the time to pack up your things. Get away from the ocean right away.

Where should you go during a tsunami? Try to get as far from the ocean as fast as you can. It is a good idea to make a plan for where you will go. That way, you will be able to act quickly if you need to.

If roads are busy, you should walk, run, or bike. Move quickly and get as high as you can. The top floor of a tall building is a good choice. Or go to the top of the highest hill in the area. Otherwise, climb a tree and hold on. If you are caught by a wave, search for something like a piece of wood to help you float.

People who survive the waves of a tsunami still need to be careful. Just inches of moving water can sweep people off their feet. Electrical power lines may be on or near the ground. These can cause electrical shocks or burns. Even something that is touching a downed power

TSUNAMI HAZARD ZONE

IN CASE OF EARTHQUAKE GO TO HIGH GROUND OR INLAND

Coastal areas with a history of earthquakes tend to be at greater risk for tsunamis.

line can hurt you. Stay away from broken gas lines, too. Leaking gas can explode. Do not go into buildings that have been damaged. Exposed nails, broken glass, and falling objects are dangerous. Stay off bridges that have been hit. Officials will let you know when it is safe to move around.

People should have an emergency kit. Pack bottled water, canned and dried food, a manual can opener, a battery-operated radio, and a first-aid kit in a waterproof bag with a handle. Keep the kit in the family car or in a closet near an exit. Everyone in the family should know where the kit is. That way, if you need to leave in a hurry, you can grab the kit and go.

The 2004 Indian Ocean tsunami left dangerous rubble across Indonesia.

CHAPTER FOUR

AFTER A TSUNAMI

A tsunami is not just one wave. It includes many waves and can last for hours. The first wave is not always the biggest. The quake's aftershocks may continue to make big waves. People should stay where they are until they hear it is safe. Officials will send information on the radio. They will let people know when the event is over. It is dangerous to return to the beach to watch the ocean. Be patient. Stay away until local officials give word.

Some survivors may not have a place to go. Waves can destroy homes. These people should listen to the local radio station for direction. Organizations that help people after a disaster often set up shelters. Shelters give people food, clean water, and a place to sleep.

Fire trucks line up to help those in need following the 2011 tsunami in Japan.

DANGEROUS BACTERIA

Bacteria are small organisms. You cannot see them. But they are in soil, water, air, and on plants and animals. About a billion bacteria live in a teaspoon of soil. Some are helpful. Others cause diseases. Bacteria need water to grow. Large waves soak areas with water. This increases the number of bacteria, which can make people sick.

Getting clean water can be difficult after a tsunami. Floodwater is usually full of dirt and debris. Insects that carry disease are drawn to standing water. People who drink or touch polluted water can become sick. Dead animals may also be in the water. Snakes may be swimming around. It is important to stay away.

It may take workers a while to bring fresh food and clean drinking water to areas with damaged roads. Some foods need to be refrigerated. Do not eat these foods if they have not been kept cold for more than a few hours. This is when emergency kits are useful. Eat canned or dry food from sealed containers. Drink bottled water.

People who are injured during a tsunami may need medical help. Minor cuts and bruises can be treated with a first-aid kit. Do not try to move a person who is hurt badly. If phone lines are working, call 911. Keep the hurt person warm and clean. Listen to the radio for information on how to get medical help.

Tsunamis can be scary. But big tsunamis are rare. Many people live with the possibility of a tsunami every day. But they do not worry. They know they will be prepared if big waves hit.

People with major injuries may go into shock. It is important to keep them calm and warm.

Glossary

debris (duh-BREE) Debris is the remains of destroyed objects. Water after a tsunami is often filled with debris.

displace (dis-PLASE) To displace is to move something from its usual location. Earthquakes on the ocean floor displace the water above.

epicenter (EP-i-sen-tur) The epicenter is the place on the earth's surface above an earthquake. Tsunamis begin in the ocean near the epicenter of an earthquake.

erosion (i-ROH-zhuhn) Erosion is the process by which something slowly wears away. After the tsunami, erosion causes soil to wash away.

faults (fawlts) Faults are cracks between plates of the earth's crust. Earthquakes occur along faults.

foundations (foun-DAY-shuhnz) Foundations are the support structure underneath buildings. Tsunamis can weaken foundations so that buildings fall down.

magnitude (MAG-ni-tood) A magnitude is a number that measures an earthquake. A 7.0 magnitude earthquake can cause serious damage.

nuclear (NOO-klee-ur) Nuclear means related to the use of atomic energy. The tsunami in Japan caused a leak in a nuclear power plant.

seismic (SIZE-mik) Seismic means caused by an earthquake. Quakes send seismic waves to the earth's surface.

To Learn More

BOOKS

Kajikawa, Kimiko. *Tsunami!* New York: Random House, 2010.

Osborne, Mary Pope. *Magic Tree House Fact Tracker #15: Tsunamis and Other Natural Disasters.* New York: Random House, 2012.

Tarshis, Laura. *I Survived the Japanese Tsunami, 2011.* New York: Scholastic, 2013.

WEB SITES

Visit our Web site for links about how to survive a tsunami:

childsworld.com/links

Note to Parents, Teachers, and Librarians: We routinely verify our Web links to make sure they are safe and active sites. So encourage your readers to check them out!

Index